WAIT FOR ME

Best wishes
Marty Gervais

Wait for Me

New poems by
Marty Gervais

Black Moss Press
2006

Published by Black Moss Press, 2450 Byng Road, Windsor, Ontario N8W3E8. Black Moss books are distributed in Canada by LitDistco in Toronto.

Library and Archives Canada
Cataloguing in Publication

Gervais, C. H. (Charles Henry), 1946-
         Wait for me / Marty Gervais.

Poems.
ISBN 0-88753-419-8

        I. Title.

PS8563.E7W34 2006   C811'.54   C2006-901817-0

Acknowledgements

My gratitude goes to my good friend, John B. Lee, for the final edit of these poems, but also to Melanie Santarossa and Nicole Koloff who first put these poems in order. The input, support and encouragement of a host of others, however, should not go unnoticed, and I count Robert Hilles, Alistair MacLeod, Roger Bell, Karen Mulhallen, Marilyn Gear Pilling, Mary Ann Mulhern and Nino Ricci among those. And special thanks to Karen Monck for her patience in getting this manuscript ready for publication.

Cover is from a photograph by Marty Gervais.
It was taken at the Musée D'Orsay in Paris.

Design by Karen Veryle Monck

For Julien, Sebastien and Calder

Table of Contents

A Child Dreams in Green

A child's drawing
shows a smiling sun
and a band of green
that runs to the river

A child's drawing
shows a dancing tree
and feet that sprint
straight into sky

A child's drawing
shows a moon that smiles
and a lonely boy who sings
in the key of green

In The Light of An Ordinary Morning

I study the ants
swarming the counter tops
in the light of an ordinary morning
Some march in single file
others in twos
Some pause momentarily
remembering suddenly
they left behind their wallet
or prescription
on the dresser at home
Some stand stock still
maybe waiting for a friend
maybe talking on the cell phone
Some scurry like they're late
for an appointment
Some walk in circles
confused and desolate over
a piece of bad news
A dab of strawberry jam
is the prize, the mother lode
It sits on the cutting board
amid toast crumbs
and the engineers are drafting
a strategy to spirit this
to the nest, to the Queen
who paces in front
of a tiny ant mirror
despairing over the weight
she's put on and what
she'll wear for the feast
celebrating their great find
I'm way ahead
I know something they don't

I know it's a matter of time
before I wreak havoc
upon this industrious colony
What shall it be?
Flood from an overturned mug?
Tsunami by wash cloth?
Death by a giant finger
flicking them into insect eternity?
Or should I be the benevolent god?
I'm way ahead —
Let them live an hour longer
while I drive to Home Hardware
and buy those tiny plastic
feeding stations
— space age looking drive-ins
I'll invite them one by one
to pull into these rest stops
along their route
to gorge themselves
on super sized meal deals
I'll give them time to go back
and tell friends
and bring the little ones,
the old, the sick
I'm way ahead of them
God is good
God is patient
God feeds his children

Taking A Drive On Summer Evenings

He tells me that
on summer evenings
he cruises by the house
owned by the man who slept
with his wife
and slows down in uncertain hope
of hearing this man's voice
through the screen door
spying him cutting
the lawn, or fixing his van
It doesn't bother him like it used to
There was a time he would avoid
driving in that end of town
take a detour
and if he had to run by the street
where this man lived
he would look the other way
maybe turn up the radio
maybe talk loudly to himself
Now he makes a point of
going out of his way
like visiting a grave site
of someone who mattered
He's never spoken to the man
never dialed his number
never written him a letter
Has no idea what he'd say
if he ever ran into him
though silently in the car
he rehearses that moment
of confrontation
There are times too when
he's written this man's name down

and stared at it, imagining
his wife with this stranger
on late winter nights
when he was out of town
recalls telephoning her once
and how agitated she was
and he wondered what he had said
to get her so upset
Or the time he got home
and the door was locked
and she came from the basement
Said she had hired a man
to fix the locks on the door
and he was now
doing repairs to the dryer
Never thought anything of it
Now he tells himself
it doesn't matter much any more
not like before, not like when
she first confessed the affair
Doesn't matter much any more
Still, as he turns down the man's street
his heart slows and those moments
thunder in his head and his car drifts
in the warm summer evening
and he imagines how easy
how quick, and how perfect
it would be to torch his house

Praying and Peeing

I am the boy
with the bird on his head
I'm peeing and this damned bird
that has come in through
an open window at the school urinals
won't budge
I wiggle and squirm
hoping erratic movements
will nudge this fluttering angel
but instead its feet shift on my head
like it's standing on a spinning globe
The other boys beside me
peeing at the row of urinals
are all laughing
I begin praying to the Blessed Virgin
Please Mary, Mother of Jesus
the ever blessed and most immaculate
most glorious beyond compare
woman without defilement
who gave birth to God, the Word,
the true mother of God
I love all living things
I know this to be God's creature
Please make this motley dove fly away
Please make these boys wet themselves
from laughing so hard
Please free me finally of these claws
that dig into my scalp
It's the least you can do
I'm peeing for heaven's sake

OATMEAL

I had trouble
with the name —
kept saying *Quack*...er
Quack...er *Quack*...er Oats
Besides why was this fellow
on the cereal box
so fat and happy?
What's with the
stupid hat and hair
that billows out the sides
like clouds in picture books?
And the red cheeks?
My dad kept joking,
"A drinking problem, maybe?"
And that tie like a barber's bib?
No one on my street
would be caught dead
dressing like this fellow
not where I lived
Every day I'd stare
at his picture on the counter top
by the big metal pot
my mother up at dawn
in a disheveled nightgown
stirring *porridge*
while everyone else
on the street
called it *oatmeal*
My mother's secret was
to drop a ridge of butter
into the bubbly oats
just before serving
and like clockwork

my brother fiddled
with the dials on the radio
till he finally tuned
in Pat Boone
then my mother would slowly
waltz that steaming pot
across the linoleum floor
crooning *April Love*
like she was on stage
At 12 she taught me
to make porridge
and now here I am filling a pot
just so, letting the water
come to a boil, adding a pinch
of salt, pouring in the oats
Now here I am, 57, up at 2 a.m.
the hum of the house
loud in my ears, I am alone
the world sleeps
I have decided to place
the package of Quaker's Oats
in front of me as I eat
in the silence
of this winter morning
I have almost forgotten
the bemused face of this man
on the cereal package
Reminds me of a boarding school
teacher — the look on his face
of someone relishing having just
caught a student cheating on
a math exam or engaged in
the act of self-abuse
I stare at the face
find myself talking to him

about my mother, boring him
with details of when things
were simple, when my mother
danced with a pot of oatmeal
when she moved with the grace
of Ginger Rogers on mornings
when it was still dark
when no one dared
take her for granted

BLOWING KISSES

My dad on a Sunday afternoon
driving his new Chev
blowing kisses at the blonde
stepping out of the diner
on Wyandotte
and she, smiling, and turning
slightly to let the wind catch her hair
Imagine my dad feeling
pretty good about himself
catching one last look
of the blonde in the rear view mirror
and blowing one last kiss
I think of the word "blowing"
the act of one that blows.
a disturbance occurring when trapped gas
or steam escapes from molten metal
a defect in china
hard breathing
and my dad hyperventilating
in his new Chev at the sight
of her, the molten
metal of the fishtail fins
gleaming in the hot sun
the disturbance around
the heart like trapped gas
Blowing in the wind
The answer my friend
is blowing in the wind
The word "blow"
<u>*Noun*</u> — *(1), a hard hit; knock; stroke.*
The boxer struck his opponent a blow
that knocked him down.
(2), a sudden happening

that causes misfortune or loss
or severe shock.——
His mother's death was a great blow
But the woman at the diner
was no misfortune, no disaster
No great blow or knock
or hard hit, except to the heart
my dad's heart soaring in his chest
that summer day when all
the world talked of Korea
and Ike played golf
The kisses blowing in the wind
The answer my friend is
blowing in the kisses
Blow and blow and blow
blowback, blow-dry, blowfly, blowhole,
blowup, blow the gaff, blowdown,
blow-by-blow, blow in, blow the whole
whistle
blow gun, blow off, blow ball, blow lamp
blowjob, blow hot and cold, blowhard
blow a person's mind
Blow and blow blow
and blow your boat
gently down the street …
and my dad's car rides
like a boat on the heat waves of suburbia
and he'll huff and he'll puff
and he'll blow the house down
<u>Blow</u>: *a sudden attack or assault.*
The army struck a swift blow at the enemy
I think of the expressions
come to blows, to start fighting
After a few harsh words
the two boys came to blows

over the sweetheart at the diner
And my dad's car rides proudly
in his big blue Chev
Blow, blow, blow
I'll huff and I'll puff and
I'll blow your house down
And the newspapers reported
a blow-by-blow account of the day
I think of my dad riding in
his big blue Chev, its fins glistening
and proud in the sunlight
I hear
blow blow blow your boat
gently down the street
I'll huff and I'll puff
And I'll huff and I'll puff
and I'll blow your house down

Chicken Coop Opera

I wake —
believing I must've
fallen asleep in a chicken coop
on my grandfather's farm
the cooing and clucking
and quick fluttering of wings
like the soft slap
of a screen door in summer
I roll over in bed
the large wooden shutters
open to the market street
sunlight of a spring day
spreading its lazy limbs
into every corner
of this high-ceilinged
hotel room in Bologna
I wake —
my right eye sunken
into a pillow
the left eye suddenly
spying a pigeon on the dresser
It's staring at me
as if I owe it house rent
What the hell! I mutter
and roll over
now spotting them —
pigeons roosting
on curtain rods, the radio
a table, lampshades, bed posts
even the toilet seat
a dozen birds now inhabiting
this room — figuring
the open window is

an invitation to this
afternoon cocktail party
in my honor
or maybe they've come
to discuss the new opera
at the concert hall down
the maze of colonnaded streets
or maybe they sensed
my loneliness for my family
across the ocean
I shut my eyes —
maybe I'm dreaming
Then again maybe not
Maybe they're dreaming
and there's a naked man rolling
about in their new home
and he won't get up to leave

The Egg

It might've been a cloudy
Thursday morning
as you made your way to school
and scooped up
a speckled blue robin's egg
that had fallen in the field
behind the house
You slipped it into your pocket
and from time to time
throughout the gloomy day
you slid a hand into the warm jacket
and cupped its subtle contours
like a pebble washed ashore
It might've been after haying
and a sky swarming
with black birds and storm clouds
that brought you by this field
and you marveled at
this feather-light egg
and took it home
and worried over its frigidity
its glossy membrane
embraced by your hand
like a secret
It might've been
you felt badly the next day
and went back to the raked
and rolling field and stood
under a wide open sky
and, open palm, held the egg up
as if it belonged among the wind
or it might've been your uncle, furious
at your laziness and daydreaming

slapped your side and ˙
broke the tiny egg
in your pocket and told you
to wake up and get back
to your chores
Or it might've been
that every now and then
when you sleep at night
the egg seems to float
in your weightless boyish dreams
sky blue and small

SOMEONE SPECIAL

Years later
when I returned to the town up north
where I had come of age
I read her obituary in the paper
She had lived till she was 62
Died of cancer
A breast removed
I never really knew her
except from the pharmacy
how she always embarrassed us
She was a little older
and whenever we sidled up to the counter
and awkwardly asked about *protection*
she knew all the slang for condoms
and she'd wink: "For someone special?
Susan? Patricia? That slut from the Hollow?
So, what will it be, boys? Love socks
the goalie, jimmy-hat, willie warmers
rubber johnnies, raincoats, the silicon
sinner, latex lover, french letters?
Speak up, boys?"
We felt like running away . . .
Today as I read the paper I recall
the first time I had seen her
or at least a picture of her
It was that first fall after we moved to town
and my Grade 7 teacher ordered me
to pry open my geometry set
that sat on the edge of my desk —
and me refusing for no good reason
and my new buddies giddy
over my defiance — but I didn't know
what they had cooked up

till I flipped open the metal case
and there resting on the stiff plastic protractor
was a snapshot of a breast
a single black and white photo scissored out
— a tit like a bull's-eye
Later in the school yard my buddies
showed me the rest of the photograph
And there she was — then a teenager
grinning at the camera, hands on her hips
topless and sassy but missing
the left breast that had now disappeared
into the teacher's desk drawer

The History of My Clothes

I dress in the dark
so as not to wake my wife
when I get up at 5 a.m.
The pants
I wore yesterday
gabardines, blue,
34 in. waist, 30 in-seam
washable — bought
at Moore's on sale
Was $78, marked down 15%
now another 30%
for the summer sale
I'll wear them again
What about a shirt?
I won't turn on the lights
in the closet — I reach
out in blackness
like a blind man
and feel the lineup
on hangers, convinced
I can match the feel
of the fabric with the colour
I've mastered this
also memorized the order
from left to right:
three shirts in, I'll find
a blue broad cloth
button down, bought
at the Bay three years ago
15 neck, 34-35 sleeve
full price $43
Next to it are two silks
tailored in Hong Kong

very blousy
I won't wear them
feel too much like Mozart
whenever I extend my arms
loose-fitting sleeves drooping
Feel the urge to play — notes
bouncing my brain and feel
I'm wearing one of those
courtly period powdered
periwigs
I settle on a shirt
counted eight from the left
a *Daniel Hechter*, button down
cotton/polyester blend
robin's egg blue
I could be a stockbroker
— I'll take risks today
buy and sell immortal souls
like Lucifer, make a fortune
for some, ruin others
But first I've got to find
some underwear —*Stanfields*
loose fitting, large
I hate anything gripping me
down there unless it's
of my own making
And my socks, black
always black — buy 10 pairs
at a time, all the same so
when they come out of the dryer
hot like croissants out of the oven
there's no worry over matching
Always the same price
three pairs, $9
cotton, stretchy

I'm ready now
I lay out the clothes on the bed
in the dark, my wife still
slumbering, first the *Stanfields*
now the socks, now the *Daniel
Hechter* and stand there a moment
feeling out of place
awkward like a hockey player
lounging about in full uniform
but without skates
Finally, the gabardines
I'm ready —
I feel like me
I am me
I'm everybody

The Sky Is Falling

If you stare
at your knees long enough
they look ridiculous
fat and wrinkled
padded ear muffs
a walnut crunch
from Tim Hortons
a sad and silly omelets
perhaps an aerial view of
Luxembourg
where I imagine people
commuting to work
reading the paper
at open air cafes
complaining about the Euro
women motoring
to work and putting
on lipstick in the car
kids skipping off to school
I want to tell them
they are all part of a new
civilization this world
of my knees, two principalities
side by side, divided
that a greater world exists
beyond, that the sky is
not falling, that they're all
related, one to the other,
the knee bone connected
from your leg bone
your leg bone connected from
your ankle bone, your ankle
bone connected from

your foot bone
to … this universe
of parts, that we function
together yet know
nothing of each other
the knee bone connected
to your thigh bone, your thigh
bone connected to the hip bone
your hip bone connected to
your back bone, your back
bone connected to your
shoulder bone, your shoulder
bone connected to your neck
bone your neck bone connected
to your head bone
and I hear the word of the Lord
I can't help but feel
the hip bone moving
in this waltz, floating
in its own world
figuring it ought to remain
independent, alone, solitary
as it swivels in this dance
of bones, as its praises
its autonomy
I stare at my knees again
wonder if they
are just knees, doughy
pads of flesh that in
my boyhood knelt
before the gods above
out of fear of a world
collapsing—
and my brain somewhere
in the midst of all this

spins like the smooth globe
at the back of the classroom
where I struggled in
Grade six to make
sense of why the nuns
shaved their heads bald

THE STORIES ABOUT US

I carried the cardboard box
from her house after she died
and placed it below
the stairs in the basement
forgot about it till now
when I was cleaning out
the space, hauling away
hockey sticks, team jerseys
old skates, baseball cards
a broken down bicycle
At first couldn't figure out
what it was doing there
what was in it
till I opened the lid —
my mother's college certificate
a picture of Da Vinci's Last Supper
that used to hang
in the family dining room
a Brownie box camera
finally her notebooks
stories she wrote
I imagined her sitting
at the edge of the dock
in a rickety lawn chair
daylight falling about her
like an exquisite dancer
slowly bowing
at the end of a performance
Imagined her lost
in stories of her youth
and my father nearby smoking
and pacing the yard
swatting at the capricious bats

darting in the diminishing light
my mother writing
at the lake house in Muskoka
All these years later
I sit on the floor
of the basement
study the long and decorative
loops of the letters
G and *H* and *A*
and wondered why I left
those notebooks unopened
and stored away
below the basement stairs
and wondered
what was I afraid of
what did I fear
why should I care

APOLOGY

In the night, I speak with you
knowing the last time I saw you
was on the fourth floor of the hospital
your gaping face reaching to
the heavens, limbs asleep
blood pooling in the sheets below
I apologize for not driving back
that hot June night as I had promised
I can't forget that early morning
a languid sun lifting itself over rooftops
of a slumbering city amid
harsh shadows of a new day
seeing you alone, the nurses gossiping
and yawning, waiting for the shift change
I sat beside you, amazed
I had nothing to say
had nothing to share with you
Instead I slumped in a chair
at the end of the bed waiting
for my brother, wondering
what a son ought to do in a room
where his mother has passed away
Fourteen years later I lie awake
hoping to speak with you
a thousand questions needing answers
all the things I couldn't say
and pray now for you to hear me
Then when I least expect it
— my mind engulfed in
bills and schedules — I catch
sight of the hem of your dress
disappearing into shadows
out of my reach

The Letters

The bachelor uncle sleeps alone
in the room
at the top of the stairs
the very room that was his as a child
I ask his nephew if he ever married
ever had a girlfriend
and so the story unfolds
the time his nephew, flipping
through old stamp collections
diaries and photo albums,
found some unopened letters
from a woman his uncle
had known at school
how one November he had
taken the sheep to show
at the Royal Winter Fair
and spotted her walking
and caught her attention
Some say he lolled about
chatting with her, catching up
finding out she had gone
to Toronto to become a nurse
The letters were bound
together with an elastic band
and in them were the apologies
about a scene made when
she invited him to her house
in the city, her boyfriend
taking exception
And the uncle — then a young man
in stiff wool suit, boots polished
hair slicked back, stood
in the parlour of her house

with a bouquet of wild flowers
gathered from the roadsides
of Kent County
and recited something
from Emily Dickinson
and embarrassed her
and himself
And another time
stopped by her house
when she wasn't there
and left a box of chocolates
at the front door
She stopped writing
after the uncle retreated
to the silence of his room
tucked away her letters
in the bottom drawer
of a dresser, never having
opened them, never
having answered them

ONE EIGHT HUNDRED

It started with a phone call
a 1-800 number
on television at 4 a.m.
Harry Lorayne's Memory Power
A short guy
with a Brooklyn accent
pacing a studio audience
inviting each one
to identify themselves
by name and occupation
By the end of the show
after he's demonstrated
tried and true techniques
of photographic memory
he's reciting back everything
they've told him
I can't sleep
I have nothing better to do
My memory is shot
My mind often goes blank
when introducing my wife
at a party, or maybe
I panic, thinking *This is stupid*
—I can't remember
her name after 30 years of marriage!
So I dial the number
I am talking to someone
on the phone who takes down
my Amex number
It's settled —
Memory Power will arrive
in five to six weeks
Fine — I go back to bed

A month or more later —
I can't remember how much
time has elapsed — I'm up
in the middle of the night
watching television and realize
Memory Power hasn't arrived
I call another 1-800 number
hoping it's the same
but truly can't remember
if it is — and tell
this telemarketer on the phone:
"I ordered a memory building
product from one of your
television shows ..."
"Do you have the product number, sir?"
"No, I don't. I can't remember it."
"Do you have the name, sir?"
"The product name? No, I don't."
"Well, sir, we need the name!"
"You see," I explain, "I ordered
this because it's supposed to help
me remember things!"
"You can't remember the name, sir?"
"That's right — that's why I need this!"
And so the conversation goes
I tell her I remember the show's host
"You know *his* name?"
"Sorry, I don't, but he was short
and talked fast and had curly hair."
"That doesn't help, sir —we need
his *name*! Well . . . perhaps you
can you tell me how long ago
you ordered this product?"
Sadly, I couldn't —
I didn't know the product name

the host's name, when
I ordered it, not even where
I put my Amex receipts ...
I did know there was snow
on the ground that morning
— it must have been winter
I did know my car wouldn't start
I did know I telephoned the Auto Club
I even remember the name
of the man who came out
to jump start my car — George —
and can't forget him telling me
his youngest daughter
went to the same school
as my boy and she was sick
that day, was throwing up
I did know a lot of things about
that day — my wife's
hair appointment, even the
time, and my oldest boy was
heading for a hockey tournament,
and my brother was going into
the hospital for more tests
I did know it was a crisp morning
I huddled in the cold
on the street beside the car
waiting for George, and
never saw him again after
that day — never even ran
into him at school
I told the telemarketer all these things
and we talked at length
She was patient and listened
I talked and talked
Told her about my kids

how many goals my son
scored last year
how my daughter
was now living in France
how I had just celebrated
30 years of marriage
— she took it all in
never once showing signs
of waning to end the conversation
Then she started about her husband
how they met at Mardi Gras
in New Orleans, a wild night
where they wound up
at an all-night diner
and talked till dawn
Now she has three boys
all in baseball, all dreaming
of being Major Leaguers
all under the age 8
So there we were at 3 or 4
in the morning playing out
our lives on the phone
to each other, all the things
we liked to do, how much
we loved our spouses, how
we'd do anything for our kids
how we wouldn't ever change
our lives — we'd do it all over again
if given the chance
I asked for her name and she told me
and I told her my name
Finally I said goodbye
That was it ...
All these years later I remember
every detail about that early morning

the time I spent on the phone
with a stranger — I imagined
she was pretty, imagined her
removing head phones
at the end of her shift and
shaking her hair loose and
reaching for her purse
in the bottom drawer of a desk
and slipping on her coat and walking
to her car and driving off — home
to her husband and getting
the children ready for school
making lunches and
kissing them goodbye
then finally climbing into bed
I think about her often
but realize after all these years
    — and I swore I'd never forget this —
I can't for the life of me
remember her name

THE HEADLESS BIRD

My friend tells me
he cut off the head
of a chicken
and the headless bird
raced down the lane
through the gate —
as if it knew exactly
where it was going
and sprinted down
the highway
toward Highgate
where it finally dropped dead
My friend tells me
it fell short of
the Guinness Book of Records
that rewarded a
headless chicken
lasting two miles
before it finally gave
up the ghost
My friend tells me
the town's folk
chased after it
laying wagers
on how far it might travel
My friend tells me
it got to the town's limits
and figured there
was no point going further
realizing maybe the worst
had already happened
realizing it had left
behind something

in all the fuss
Meanwhile why is it
no one ever asks
about the head
left behind?
What about the
scared sad eyes of the bird?
That stunned look
and sense of panic
like on someone's face
who anxiously fumbles
for a set of keys lost
in a coat pocket
or left on the piano
by the door
Meanwhile there is
that silly puny head
inching its impotent way
still clacking
"Wait for me!
Wait for me!
Wait for me!"

LOSING A BRAIN

This guy beside me
at the lunch counter
tells me his friend doesn't blink
I tell him he's lying
On the average people blink 12 times a minute
and if you were awake for 14 hours a day
you'd blink 10,080 times
and if you lived till 85
and were awake 14 hours a day on average
you would blink 856,800 times
I study his friend's eyes
tell him to remove his glasses
notice a severe case of acne
a prominent nose
a scar over the left eyebrow
how the whites of his eyes are red
I stare at him for a couple of minutes
and unless he was blinking
at the same time as I was
then maybe it's true —
he doesn't blink
I stare at him in silence
The fellow next to me is smiling
like he just won a bet
I ask his buddy if he sleeps with his eyes open
He swears he never shuts his eyes day or night
I ask how can that be
The guy beside me interrupts —
most birds sleep with one eye open
the other shut
and that a scientific study found
mallards sleep about 86 per cent of the time
with one eye open

but it was always birds on both ends
of a row, not those in the middle,
that slept this way, probably
out of fear for predators
and didn't show a preference
for which eye they kept open
It was never the same
and while sleeping, one hemisphere
of the brain was awake, the other snoozing
The guy beside me went on to say penguins sleep
side by side in a zoo in New York with eyes open
and how once he spotted a cockatiel
slumbering in front of a mirror
with the eye away from the mirror open
as if its reflection was another cockatiel
He swears dolphins, whales, seals
and manatees are also half-sleep presumably
to permit them to surface for air while sleeping
I tell him he's lying again
and I can't keep my eyes off his friend
I rub my eyes till they're red
I know this guy's lying
"Are you shitting me?" I ask
I mean, this guy's gotta blink,
he's gotta, and the more I stare at him
the more I find myself blinking
"You're kidding, right?" I ask
but no one's answering
I take off my glasses in defeat
I tell his friend
 "Look, I know one thing —
you're no goddam bird!"

FINDING THE INDIAN OCEAN

He had always wanted to dip
his toe into the Indian Ocean
travelled thousands of miles
to South Africa to stay with an aunt
planned to motor to the ocean
but she told him it was dangerous
he ought to stay close
ought not venture too far
Instead, he dreamed
of the ocean 300 miles away
his mind swarming with memories
of his youth, a summer
when he swam out into Lake Erie
to fetch a cow that had toppled in
and drifted out, how he led her
back to shore, this big hulking wet heifer
Observed it standing on the shore
shaking itself free of lake water
seeing it waltz across the sandy beach
like a fat woman at a barn dance
searching for a partner
He had always wanted to dip
his toe into the Indian Ocean
and all one afternoon pored
over encyclopedias and maps
and day-dreamed of that moment
made a half dozen calls
to touring groups
finally giving up when he was told
it could not be done
and he lay there on a couch
by the window, the soft afternoon

light falling over him
like the sweet voice of a country tune
He had always wanted to dip
his toe into the Indian Ocean
but instead went out to buy
post cards and guide books
and spent his time driving into town
idling in coffee shops, reading
the paper and talking to locals
He finally told a truck driver
who sat down beside him
at the counter
how he had wanted to make
that trek to the Indian Ocean
if only to dip his toe into its waters
Weeks later sitting by the window
at his aunt's house
a truck pulled up to the house
at the edge of town
— that same man
wearing a wide-brimmed hat
got out and made his way to the door
carrying with him a bucket
that sloshed with water
and handed it to my bewildered friend
who asked what this was all about
And the man holding the bucket
spoke about having just come
from the Indian Ocean
how he had slipped
the plastic container into it
and drove straight back to this house
My friend then pealed off his socks
dipped his toes into the bucket of water
and with eyes shut imagined himself

slowly wading into the open ocean
on a cool morning in July
and turning to his wife
said, "It's not so cold, honey —
once you get in."

READING GLASSES

My wife keeps losing
her reading glasses
Buys them by the dozen
knowing if she has misplaced them
they'll be in any one
of a dozen places —the car
kitchen countertop
bathroom commode
near the phone
on the patio table
in any one of four
or five purses
maybe in a winter coat
maybe in the pocket
of a blazer
My wife keeps losing
her reading glasses
She doesn't seem to worry
— they'll turn up
yet she keeps searching for them
usually clutching in one hand
the thing she needs to read
those few lines of a note
left out for her
maybe a telephone number
or recipe or bank statement
My wife keeps losing
her reading glasses
She drives to Zellers
finds a prescription
that fits her eyes
and strolls out in

the afternoon sunlight
with the new pair
tucked away in a purse
in a place she's certain
to find them the
next time she picks up a book
My wife keeps losing
her reading glasses
I can't help but watch her
as she frantically
searches for them
when she's handed a menu
I can't help but imagine
a dozen pairs
folded up and asleep
like tiny quiet birds
awaiting her call

WE ALL KNEW
For D.P.

When things were going wrong
You'd tell your friends
you were heading north
then drive a mile and a half
— south actually —
and check into the Kenora Motel
empty change from your pockets
along with a Bic lighter
a pack of *Players,* gas receipts
a flattened leather wallet
given to you by one of
the kids at a Christmas
you don't remember much about
You were probably drunk
or wished you were
When things were going wrong
you'd stand at the window
of the Kenora Motel
and study the traffic
for hours on end
— truckers edging their way
to the Ambassador Bridge
and you'd imagine yourself
running out to the street
and hailing one of them down
so you might hitch a ride
and cannonballing it to Florida
or Georgia or Alabama
or wherever — it didn't matter
You'd stand at the window
of the Kenora Motel
believing there was another life

out there to live
After a while you'd slump
at the edge of the bed
knowing you'd do nothing
to change things
then you'd dial your wife
and when she picked up
the phone you'd hang up
figuring you had nothing
more to say — you had said
it all — *what's the point?*
And so you'd sit there
in the motel darkness
except for the television glare,
the sound turned down,
and the bathroom light
filling one end of the room
You'd sit with your
old friend, Johnny Walker
drinking straight from the bottle
and cursing everybody
mostly yourself — especially
because you told everybody
you were going north
Funny thing is, we all knew
We'd see your parked car
sometimes the curtains yanked
haphazardly across the window
soft glow of the hockey game
on the tube … We all knew
you'd driven a mile and a half
from home, that you'd spotted
the sign for the Kenora
and grunted, "That's north enough!"
We all knew …

THE GRANDFATHER CLOCK

With the coming of summer
the days are longer
It takes till well past
9:30 at night
before I see reflections
of the living room
that form in the backyard window
at the far end of the house:
the fringed shade of an antique lamp
distorted —in a blur
as if someone had smacked it
as if my vision was failing
I see the edge of a picture frame
whose image has faded into
a pattern of abstracted shadows
There's a figure— maybe my wife
or son — that moves
for an instant and is gone
A grandfather clock
sitting high and proud on the wall —
its hands ticking backwards
in this mirror-like rendering
I'd like to believe I'm younger
watching these hands turn
back, marveling at every hour
spinning into decades past
where I can return
to make wiser investments
pay off the mortgage
and where after 30 years of marriage
I can bridge broken silences
heal unkind words
where I can live for the moment

make wishes and promises
I know I can keep
but where most of all
I can be with my ailing father
when he dies —as he did years ago
in a city hospital
when none of his children
were there to say
goodbye

CUTTING THE LAWN

Maybe you didn't understand your uncle's letter —
him writing about starting the lawnmower
how he had spotted you driving up the lane
getting out, going into the farmhouse
at Highgate weeks after your father's funeral
You sat at the table by the window
with your mother, and a while later
your uncle finally came into the house
climbed the stairs to his room
at the beginning of a hot spring
changed his shirt, lay the wet shirt
on the bed thinking he might get to it later
then went back out to start the lawnmower
but it was giving him trouble
and long after you had left
he had finally got it started
and finished the lawn, but sat down
and wrote this letter
about how your mother had already mowed
the lawn four days before
but here he was going at it again
and talked about the puff of black smoke
that issued from the carburetor
after he got it going, talked about
the wet grass, trouble getting through it
You wondered what was on his mind
what all this chatter was about
what he *really* meant
and you searched the letters that looped
all over the page, hen scratch
You didn't get it, did you?
It was really for him, your father
and it was telling him he was keeping busy

he was making do, the farm was okay
though the buildings needed painting
though the land needed new life
though the boots at the side door
that once belonged to him
could never be filled, not the way
they used to be, not the same
and you didn't see that

PICTURES IN THE SHRINE AT CHAMAYO

I can smell the flowers
when I step into this
mission church…
See a woman kneeling
at the communion rail
She has just tucked
a photograph of her brother
into the corner of a
framed holy picture
a brother who died
of cancer two weeks ago
a brother who had
helped her across the
border from Mexico
four years ago, drove
her in a 1972 Ford pickup
at night, helped settle
her into a small house
here, helped her
find a job cleaning
the church, doing
laundry for the priest
cooking … Now she
prays for her brother's soul
her hands wrapped
in beads, lips
trembling, and there's
her brother's picture
high up above
a tiny side altar
tucked in with a
picture of a saint
a smiling man of 45

from a time when
he knew nothing of
death, sickness
tragedy ... He knew
life, and took the risk
to bring his sister
and her children here
drove them 378 miles
mostly at night on
empty Mexican
highways ... His sister
sitting up front with
him in the cab with
an infant wriggling
the other kids cocooned
in blankets in the back
of the truck, fallen asleep
under the moon-filled
night ... She thinks about
that now and sobs knowing
the risks he took, knowing
she could never repay
him except for this
— to pray for him
to place his picture there
among the saints ...

UNDER THE WEIGHT OF HEAVEN

You sleep in the tool shed
by the road under the stars
at the back of the monastery
and tell me about the lovers
— the farm boys
with their sweethearts
who steal into the night
when all is asleep here
and park their cars
in the holy stillness
and after a while
quietly drive back out
to the highway
You hear their cars
mounting the hill beyond
and hear them disappear into
the splendid darkness
You sleep in the tool shed
by the road under the stars
and awake suddenly to
an unfamiliar sound
on the road
and look up and see
the enormous shape
of a horse like a mountain
emerging from the mist
in the early morning
but only a horse
a mare that has strayed from
a nearby farm
It lolls about
under the swaying weight
of the heavens

You sleep in the tool shed
by the road
under the stars
and wake to the morning
with the bells beckoning you
to vigils — then you see
this work horse lying
in the dark meadow
and nod to her as you would
a friend, and say good morning
then make your way to chapel
You sleep in the tool shed
under the stars
where the world
comes to you
— silent guests who steal away
your sleep, who leave you
wondering, who leave you
undisturbed, alone
You sleep in the tool shed
under the weight of Heaven ...

SUMMER BIRD SONGS

Every summer we drove north
to a cabin by Three Mile Lake
I'd sit on the dock in the morning
study the fishermen swing
tackle boxes and rods
into the dew-laden calm
see them shove out into stillness
mist rising, my children asleep
in tangled blankets of bunk beds
this, the most perfect time of day
even the reassuring putt-putt
of outboard motors shattering the silence
Slowly the bird songs would come
back to life in trees bordering
this morning lake
I'd spread out the guide books
on the cedar planks of this dock
desperately trying to make
this connection to nature
— plants and wild flowers
I rarely ever identified or remembered
from one summer to the next
the birds I could never spot
songs I could never recognize
One book suggested translating
their songs into familiar phrases
like *Pleased to meetcha, Miss Beecher!*
Pleased to meetcha, Miss Beecher
to describe the chestnut-sided warbler
or *Quick! Three beers! Quick! Three beers!*
from the olive-side flycatcher
or how about the red-eyed vireo
with *Here I am. Look at me. I'm up here!*

Here I am. Look at me. I'm up here!
Or try the yellow warbler: *Sweet, sweet,*
I'm so sweet! Sweet, sweet, I'm so sweet!
Sweet, sweet, I'm so sweet!
Or how about the California quail?
Chi-ca-go! Chi-ca-go! Or the Golden-crowned
Sparrow? *Oh dear me! Oh dear me!*
Or the Carolina wren: *Teakettle,*
Teakettle, teakettle!
I couldn't be bothered with such tips
Instead I sailed through the morning
blissfully ignorant, content to permit
the rich cacophony of sound
to wash over me time and time again

Nothing Left To Do
For John B. Lee

Your forehead and eyes swim
in the dirty rear view mirror
of the Bonneville
as it moves lazily
in the afternoon swelter
of Alabama —
I sit in the back seat
and hear your voice
saying you never make left turns
I watch your hands caress
the steering wheel
your eyes in the mirror saying *see*
and I see the hood
of the automobile turn
and turn — trained always
to go right, to spin
like the earth around the sun
or better still, like
a dog chasing its tail
We're not getting any closer
The car moves like
a continent sliding freely
into position
Even your eyes in the mirror
shift to the right, even
your right shoulder dips
down at every turn
and the Bonneville glides
instinctively like a dancer
never losing step
But where are we going?
I follow your eyes

as they search for openings,
streets, ramps, exits, anything
to receive us and the car
keeps on circling like
a somnambulist chasing a dream
But where are we going?
I imagine turning and
turning till we run straight off
the horizon, till we tumble
off the earth, till we fool ourselves
into going left
all the time swearing up
and down it's right
it's right, it's right

Breathing Sweet Hope

I sit in my car
by the side of the road
watch the combine
shave this field of winter wheat
golden and flat under a dreamy
dark summer sky
I am going to make some changes
That farmer will be my grandfather
he will float over
this landscape — straw hat
coveralls, pipe clenched
in his teeth
I will have him wave to me
from where I sit at the road's edge
I will shift the barns
and chicken coop and outhouse
closer to the house
haul out the wagons
and have my grandfather lead
the work horses into the farm yard
I will put back the oak trees
cut down years ago
in that empty pasture
where we picnicked after church
I will be six again
lumber in a summer storm
and hurry my grandmother
across the yard to shut
the enormous barn doors
against wind and rain
I will put laughter
back into her mouth
as she scoops up my limp body

that has collapsed abruptly
because the sky has erupted
into sudden thunder
I will paint reflections
in her glasses that show
wind swept trees
and spooked barn owls
as we race back to the house
I will exchange the words
in my grandfather's frown
as he stands by the back steps
to tell my mother
who has driven an hour
in the still-dark morning
to hear him say:
"Ta mere est morte."
Instead, my grandmother
will be in the kitchen
loading the wood stove
and turning to my mother
and holding her for that instant
I will stop time
— here and now — to move
all these pieces into place
the perfect farm life
in this imagined game
I will open the eyes of those I love
and breathe sweet hope
into their limbs and words
I will let prayers
finally have their day

THE TAO OF COWS
For Marilyn Gear Pilling

The white cows lie in the dark fields
tired of fences, tired of passing cars
tired of the menu of meadows
tired of shooing flies with their tails
A distant storm blinks over the hills
like a bully striding across a school yard
The cows shrug
Weather is never their friend
There's nowhere else to go
nothing to do but sleep and dream
under the summer stars
I want to tell them
from this side of the fence
how lucky they are —
no car payments, no mortgages
bills, schedules, worries
distant wars, infidelities
or lies or the death of friends
or the sins of pride
or finding excuses to leave a party
or arguments that end in bitterness
I want to tell them
from this side of the fence
I envy their Tao, their chi
their simplicity and the way they move
or shift like the clouds above
I want to tell them
from this side of the fence
they are angels in white —
fat angels maybe —
but still angels
and it's alright to be lazy

to be sleepy, to do nothing
but drift and dream
under this French sky
because they are undulating angels
in white who move with grace
and love the world
and can do nothing wrong
nothing

Knowing the Dancer from the Dance

The Cuban boxers were
lolling about the fenced yard
— tall and wearing
jackets in the heat
the faint breeze
of the Pacific wafting in
They were laughing at a young
man in a nearby café
who was putting the make
on a dark-haired woman
twice his age
and they called to her
and pointed at themselves
and laughed again
at the frustrated man
who finally tossed
a bunch of roses into the street
and stormed off
With that, one of the boxers —
urged on by the others —
galloped across the street
scooped up the flowers
and offered them to the
woman who sat for a moment
— only for a moment —
then smiled, cocked her head
in a petulant way, paused
then slowly wrapped her arms
around the boxer's neck
and kissed him on the lips
holding it a moment
— only a moment —
then gently all in one

motion, pulled away,
rose from her chair,
reached for the small cloth
handbag at the edge of
the table, and turned
and walked away
— the Cuban left as stunned
and bewildered as if
he had been caught by left hook
he never saw coming

The Outdoor Barbers

I see them in Beijing
cutting hair on the boulevard
in cool morning light
as men and women
in cars or on bicycles
make their way to jobs
as children traipse off to school
The barbers stand
under the ginkgo trees along
this noisy thoroughfare
awaiting customers who will pause
and take their place in wooden chairs
placed helter-skelter and these men
with scissors and straight razors
fan out the bib-like cloth
and for a moment it is miraculous
the way this white apparition
catches in the wind — rounded
and smooth like the top of an apple pie
If you listen closely
you will hear the quick metal scissors
amid the din in the street
like the incessant complaint of birds
the snipping dance about heads of men
who sit patiently, some
even trying to read the paper
as the work is being done
I watch the hair tumble around
their shoulders, eventually
drifting to the street
I imagine the wind catching the hair
seeing it ride in the chilly morning
and wonder about it, how it might

graze the cheek of a young girl
who will brush it away
without thinking of its origins
how this hair might drift all day
long high above chimneys
and office towers, seeking a resting place
how it might coast through
an open window and collect
on an altar of burning incense
how it might float for days
and catch on the cotton sleeve
of a street cleaner or settle
on a statue of Mao and find its way
over miles to the Great Wall
finally how it might refuge
in a cafe maybe in a bowl of soup
where an annoyed customer might
summon a waiter and point to
its presence lying there curled
and warm amid vegetables and fat
and see the waiter whisk
the bowl away and dump it

A MAN KILLING A FLY

It seems ludicrous
this would annoy me —
I find myself perched
on the can in the bathroom
with darkness filling the house
after a July thunder storm
and this fly buzzes about
I'm thinking as a boy
my hands were so quick
I could scoop flies out of the air
cup them in my palm
feel them nudge and bounce
feel the power in those seconds
before setting them free
I try again — now a grown man
but my hands thrash
at this damn fly as it circles
like a Messerschmitt
searching for greater challenges
I figure if I wait long enough
it will tire and land
then I'll nail it good
I wait and wait till I no longer
hear it spinning about
then spot it idling
on the door frame
and slowly lift up
from the toilet seat —
gripping shorts in one hand
an L. L. Bean catalogue in the other
— I'm too anxious
and begin swatting the air again
wildly missing my target

and once again must sit and wait
and chart the course
of this infuriating insect
as it soars away to the ceiling
I sit and wait and wait
and remind myself *be patient*
breathe, breathe
one, two, three, breathe
be patient — then hear it
and can't resist and
madly clobber the dead air
of the room
with this catalogue
each time this fly strafes
into my sphere
breathe, breathe
one, two, three, breathe
It's useless but I figure
I might get lucky
on one of its incessant sorties
I stand there— pants
looped around my ankles
stand there by the toilet—
naked from the waist down
pathetic and fixated —
a lonely figure
loath to surrender
like Hollywood's King Kong
— driven mad and wearily pawing
the night sky for
those insufferable planes

THE RED RIBBON
for George E. Lee

I have tucked this red ribbon
inside my black notebook
jottings about life
on the hospital ward
the nurses
visits from the surgeon
advice from the nutrionist
I scribble out all the meds
given me, the frequency
potential side effects
Note all the blood work
done, the CT scan
small bowel X-rays
white blood cell scans
The red ribbon sits there
day after day — sent to me
by a Highgate sheep farmer
as a bookmark
First prize
Wallacetown Fair
Doesn't say which year
Doesn't say for what
I never win first prize
only ever second or third
or worse honourable mention
A watercolour when I was eight
fetched honourable mention
at the C.N.E.
It was dreadful —
a picture of a fellow fishing
along the Detroit River
He looked disfigured

Judges deemed it "inventive"
Now I have a first prize ribbon
from a town I know nothing about
a fair I've never been to
First prize
a shiny red ribbon
I imagine wearing proudly
strolling amid the bustle
of farmers and housewives
flashing my first prize ribbon
pacing aisles of the best
apple pie, largest pumpkin
longest cucumber
standing about as 4-H club boys
and girls guide sheep and cows
one by one to parade
in the sunlit show grounds
of Wallacetown —
A Ferris wheel spins against
the blue sky, balloons
drift above the din
I walk about with my red ribbon
first prize winner
top of my class
best of the best
my chest sporting the purest
red flower of Agricultural Fairs
I saunter into an exhibition hall
with rows and rows of cages
— chickens and roosters
winners and losers
red, blue and yellow ribbons
festooned like Christmas lights
to narrow cages —
I think this is me

I walk about with my red ribbon
till I spot the losers — big sad eyes
of these birds
bewildered also-rans
melancholy shut-ins
and know I am one of them
I pick the best of the worst
— a dull white hen
with a gimpy leg
I love her eyes
mawkish and anxious
like women on 1960s
television's *Queen for a Day*
I love her eyes
and when she turns away
I quietly affix this radiant red ribbon
to her rickety cage

REAL AND ALIVE

Days when I dream of
you, there riding that lemon
yellow Mercedes in a hot
July night, music of Jimi
Hendrix thundering among
street lamps and trees
your hair a yellow apparition
in the sizzling darkness
I wonder about
the last moment
together at Christmas
32 years ago
your body, a gift in
the shimmering magical
night, how we told
each other we had come
to an end, finished our lives
separately
I headed south
to the border
landing a job in
a newsroom of
a daily, writing about
farm auctions, covering
the Lions Club, the
conservation authority
village councils, fall
fairs, hockey games
the poetry of every
day, and how I thought of
you, how I had once
placed such a high
value on words

that I could barely
write anything at
all those lazy afternoons
in that last summer
together, how I had
wasted my days
sleeping, how I
had squandered
everything that might
have been good and
real and alive in
us, and how after
you left, I was renewed

A MAN PEEING ON THE TRAIN

It's like trying to hit a moving target
as you plant your feet
the landscape sliding
like a fun house floor
beneath you
as you ride southern Ontario
pee streaming into the toilet bowl
sloshing with dull green water
Nothing philosophical
about this — you simply steady
your balance, ponder
the towns that pass beneath
your feet, the town
fathers who made the laws
and the mothers who raised their kids —
baker, banker, lawyer, teacher
plumber, pipe-fitter
Sunday preacher
I stand on this moving
train pissing on all of them
one by one
and they don't
even know my name

Make Believe

He'll be three in August
and has two friends
we can't see —
they're over there
one cross-legged
in the corner near the toys
the other on a chair
munching crackers
at least that's what he tells us
and when my daughter
is feeling low because
of a miscarriage
her son opens the palm
of his tiny right hand
and offers her the baby
gently cradled there
and she thanks him
and pretends to take
the infant into her own
and her son warns her
to be careful
and she promises
and he says his friends
can help — they're over there
both now eating apples
and can't you see them
can't you hear them
I want to tell my daughter
the morning she was born
I made my way down
the flight of stairs
from the dark attic flat
and carried a blanket

to wrap her in
and prayed a silent prayer
for her safety and for
all those invisible angels
that gathered silently
in the light of dawn

SEVEN SECONDS OF WISDOM

Every seven seconds
I'm promised lusty images
and only 10 feet away
a woman rolls over on her back
on a cotton beach towel
— naked breasts upturned
and praising the heavens above
So casual is she with that cell phone
I fall asleep on straw mat
snoring the afternoon away
yet my mind swarms with images
of topless women shopping
I worry for no good reason —
I dream of women idling over
cute little bottles of Dijon mustard
or fine linens or leather sandals
dream of following them down aisles
trailing after them to parking lots
dream of sitting in the backseats of cars
spying them putting on lipstick
fixing their hair in rearview mirrors
all the while topless and free
It makes me worry for bra makers
forced to make layoffs
and pine for an end to bra advertisements
and the absence of pages devoted
in the Sears catalogue to bras
and those images of perky young women
resting on the edges of beds
chatting on the telephone
lounging about in locker rooms
with other women, casual
and indifferent in bras and panties

maybe conferring about a downturn
in the real estate market
or whether they should order Thai food
Yes, I worry for the bra makers
and lament the new meaning
this brings to one-piece bathing suits
I agonize for the feminists too
when they run out of bras to burn
or bra fitters and their disappearing art
When I finally wake under a blue sky
I yearn to tell the woman near me
all I've learned
in my seven seconds of wisdom

August 14, 2003, 3:26 P.M.
For Julien Patrice

An hour after your birth
all the power
shut down in the city
And the whole
eastern seaboard
went black
Fires broke out
in Hydro-electric plants
in New York and Niagara
ABC News reported
an explosion on the sun
Other networks
blamed terrorists
Some believed it was
the end of the world
For you, it was the beginning
The hospital was shut
to the public, and
operated on emergency power
Security guards barred
the doors, admitting no one
I couldn't see you
Not just yet
For you, this was the beginning
And I'm told you lay
in my son's arms
asleep, tiny dark eyes awash
in an unfamiliar landscape
Life was at a standstill
everywhere else
Yet you grew
You grew

And you slept in my son's arms
as he cradled and walked you
in that moment
down hospital corridors
and you dreamed
your first real dreams
in the calm
of those first hours
I wasn't allowed to see you
but I imagined the world
brightening like a halo
around you
in all that puzzling darkness

Light in August

For Calder

I walked into the street
outside the hotel —
memories of those first days
in Toronto, the Roncesvalles streetcar
grinding its way past
green grocers, bakeries, butcher shops
I was starting life
a few bucks in my pocket
a vinyl suitcase with two clean shirts
A boy in search of adventure
And now I'm staying over night
down the street from
where my first born
has given birth to hers
a boy wakened by the sounds of the CNE
planes thundering overhead
on a hot day in August
I don't even know this tiny boy
whose voice carries the day
yet I want to hold him
to carry him to the balcony
to hold him and let him touch
a warm night full of stars
to hold him and let him hear
the first rumbling of nearby streetcars

April 11, 2005 6:35 A.M.
For Sebastien

Reading in the bathtub
when just down the street
you were finding your way
into the world
a month early
I was reading
about the Pope's death
Jane Fonda's facelift
A morning with
not a trace of a cloud
a blue sky smiling
3 days after my dad's birthday
a red-haired kid
who looks like his brother
arms clawing the air
waiting for hellos

PLAYING BLIND

I am told I will be blind in six months
if I don't have laser surgery
I figure I'll need practice
I shut my eyes and shuffle
about this large two-storey house
stumble into door frames
knocking over flower vases
run my head into open cupboard doors
I'm playing blind man
I shut my eyes
and make this journey through a house
I've lived in for 13 years
touching my way in this silly odyssey
trying to understand
what might befall me —
I wonder if I'll ever get used to
not reaching for my glasses
I've worn since I was six
I shut my eyes
and move timidly through
this large house,
trying to imagine colours
reds and greens and blues
the bright winter wheat
so green in those first days of spring
now turning a rich brown
in late afternoon haze …
imagine a yellow school bus
on a road maybe a mile
away across an empty field
where the barns seem to float
bobbing on the horizon
like aimless fishing boats

the sweet reds glowing
under a cerulean blue sky
I move like a somnambulist
in a cluttered landscape
that has turned me
into a stranger, an intruder
I move down corridors
refusing to give in,
pushing myself from room to room
the flat of my right hand
tracing edges and corners
my feet moving as if shuffling
along an unfamiliar lake bottom
I'm playing blind man in a game
I can't lose, for all I need do is
open my eyes —the truest of all miracles
I make my way into the bathroom
and stand before the toilet
wonder if I'll ever be able to pee
straight again —
I feel my way down basement stairs
hear the rage of a storm outside my
windows
the television news, a creaking
on an upstairs floor, the livingroom clock
I count the chimes and do the math
knowing how long
I've been playing this game
I finally land upstairs in my bedroom
rest on the edge of my bed
marvel at the darkness —
swear I can see fireflies or splashes
of light from flickering, distant lightening
Swear I can reach out
and touch it with my bare hands